A Positively Healthier Lifestyle

—

A
Positively
Healthier
Lifestyle

by Mark McIntyre

A Positively Healthier Lifestyle
Written by Mark McIntyre February 2013
First published February 2013
Edited July 2013

Mark has worked with a vast range of clients, all with their unique needs.

Over time, Mark has helped many people increase their fitness and confidence through physical activity, diet and well-being. This book gives you a refreshingly down to earth approach with the 'look good and feel good' industry, allowing you to make better life choices, not through fear, but because those choices add something to your life.

We live in interesting times where people have much less disposable income, in many cases this can ironically lead to cutting back on the type of personal investment that makes you feel great about yourself, as such, the first thing that you're likely to drop are things like the gym or your personal trainer, possibly abandon the personal ideals of local organic food and even reduce the social activities which drive your positivity, confidence and personal mental balance in general.

At exactly the same time, as abandoning the good, many embrace the negative patterns of increasing their consumption of alcohol and fast food.

This can be a precursor to drug dependency due to a negative frame of mind – Preventative and positive steps must be taken to maximise your sense of self appreciation.

This has lead Mark to write and publish this book to help you buck that trend, turn the tide and find a range of solutions that can help you become more positive than ever.

With zero preaching or assumption making, my open minded approach is what makes the methods within, extremely easy to absorb.

A Positively Healthier Lifestyle
Written by Mark McIntyre February 2013

Contents

Exercise introduction

    Connections

    Consequences of lethargy

    Worth the time and energy

    In the net ! focussing on goals

        Goals can be a reminder of the current

        Who is the goal for?

        Why those goals?

    No pain no gain

    Gym-Haters paradise

        Community centre

        Outdoor group fitness

        workout videos / home gym

        Going for a run

It doesn't seem to be working out

Too late to motivate?

A Positively Healthier Lifestyle

Overview

Overview of a positively healthier life

From the moment you escape the womb you're relentlessly targeted with messages on how to conform to a standard in every facet of your life, these messages become more and more demanding of you as you get older.

This mass media propagated information tends to be conflicting at best, this can be incredibly confusing... this diet works - it no longer works, do this to be happier - but it's a bit risky, 6 pack miracle - but it means starving to death! Does any of that sound familiar?

Whenever you open a magazine or turn on the TV, you're subjected to a relentless assault of the perfect life and body, this includes hidden and open messages which tell you that to be truly happy, successful, sexy and positive, you must buy this brand of smelly stuff, exercise like Mr or Mrs six pack at the gym, eat that lower energy snack and rather bland ready meal etc. If you fail to buy into 'the dictated dream', you may be rendered as worthless as the latest celebrity who's just been photographed with ever so slightly wobbly legs, or a less than perfect bottom which is plonked in 'that' car, phah!

In short, you're made to feel less worthy if you don't

fully commit to the prescribed ideals as laid out by the media. There has to be more to it, right?

Mental wellbeing is often ignored and when it becomes too much to ignore, it's then brushed under the carpet or casually managed with drugs of ever increasing dosages.

Mental health aka wellbeing, seems to be an explosive subject, especially in the UK where people fear being stigmatised. Those that do seek to enhance their wellbeing and inner energy are often derided as being some sort of 'new age and out there' weirdo, thus a genuine pursuit of wellbeing is often abandoned.

Very few professionals discuss the clear and vital connection between exercise, nutrition and wellbeing in a more profoundly joined up method; instead these are generally split up and commonly treated in isolation from each-other, for example;

1. Are you going through emotional trauma?
You could be referred to a counsellor
2. Are you overweight or have an eating disorder?
You could be sent o the dietician
3. Are you physically unfit?
The gym seems the obvious solution.

The single solution / isolated process could prove detrimental in the longer term. It might well be better to understand how the body and mind work better within a more joined-up mental and physical approach to enhancing well-being.

In this marketing derived pop culture world, wellbeing is assaulted by a relentless tirade of emotive marketing campaigns which play on three crucial elements; sex, loss and success.

Everybody fears loss, most people submit to the promise of sex and the lure of success is encouraged by all sides.

This barrage of advertising funnels us into an existence where, through those three elements, we work hard on how we appear to others on the outside, while ignoring what makes us happy and healthy for ourselves on the inside.

We're often reminded that, *'beauty comes from within'*, this from the very people who focus on the superficial 'without'.

To have clear skin, strong hair, good teeth, bright eyes, to feel more energetic, enjoy a stronger sense of motivation, higher positivity, a great body, clarity of thought, to be more successful, ambitious and great company in a strive to be the best you can be, that comes from within, not some beauty cream or any quick fix formula.

This book is the result of personal life experiences as a personal trainer and some might say, idealist, I am not using others findings or feeding you into any fixed aspect of the diet or fitness industry.

Instead I'm conveying a variety of solutions which have worked with my clients over the last ten years or so. Many of the approaches might be considered 'common sense', but this presents that 'common sense' in a way that empowers you to making better decisions that enhance you.

It's really important for you to realise that you're unique, what works for you might not work for someone else.

Within this book, you're presented with options, only by trying something different will you achieve all of what you want from your life. If you take just one thing from it, then that one thing can be the seed to personal growth, a stronger sense of self determination and greater personal confidence.
If you read this and gain nothing from it, then I congratulate you on living a life in excellent balance.

Remember that the world does not owe you anything, but it wants to give you everything, it can only do that once you accept yourself as being amazing.

Doing nothing is easy. Taking that first step in a new direction is brave and many 'friends' will tempt you to stop. Choosing your own path takes courage but the rewards are tremendous, because of this, some people might, though their own insecurities try to convince you that 'standard' is the best way for you... I say to you, *'knowledge supplies you with the power and will to realise your true potential'*.

The big benefits of positivity

Enhanced psychological and physical well-being.
Better able to cope with demanding situations.
More likely to be successful in your career.
Happier family life.
Increased life span with greater quality of life.
Lower rates of depression and distress.
Stronger immune system - less prone to illness.
Reduced risks of heart attack.
Better managed weight
Improved posture
Stronger 'will' to complete personal challenges

Plus so many more enhancements to your life.

The positive way ahead

Look at any raging inferno, you could say that it's having a whale of a time on its personal journey of growth, lighting up any room it enters and burning brightly, but what does this fire require to survive and thrive?
Fire needs just three things to thrive, I'm sure you were taught this elemental lesson in school, often taught as the fire triangle, the fire triangle, at a glance, shows you what any standard carbon based fire requires to thrive ;

Heat
Fuel
Oxygen

If any part of the fire triangle fails, the fire is extinguished.

The system of achieving a more positive life is similar to the fire triangle in that you're only required to consider three elements, these must work together to achieve the effect. More of this shortly.

Humans, as a race are supremely intelligent, quite possibly due to this intelligence we find it devilishly straightforward to invent reasons why we *must* be unhappy, to aid that we make sacrifices and live a life we feel is a lie.

We often come to these conclusions thanks to a whole variety of influences ;

* Conflicting Information by the media
* Gradual brainwashing via adverts
* Key decisions being taken from you
* Becoming a victim to corporate greed
* Impossible idols - Airbrushed dream
* Negativity around you
* Being told by media that you're a failure
* Comparing physical make up to others
* The illusion of what true personal success is
*

There is a better where you are in control and enjoy ;
* Health and fitness
* Motivation
* Happiness
* Personal achievement

This book is designed to help you accept the concept that a healthier and happier life is so much easier to achieve than the media may have you believe, so use your supreme intelligence to form more positive thoughts and actions.

Like the fire triangle, positivity requires just three elements to work in harmony.

* Nutrition.
* Fitness.
* Mental wellbeing.

If you eat well, exercise and feel positive about work, friends, family etc then everything else you want from life will fall into place without any other action required.

So, bin the scales, throw away the BMI chart, jump off the diet bandwagon and start to feel much more confident and sure about yourself, knowing that you're in control of what you do, how you feel and act though internal factors and external influencers.

In other words, free yourself and be yourself.

So, as previously mentioned, this can all seem to be a common sense approach to 'self help'. By that I mean that it isn't preachy or unnecessarily jingoistic.

This book helps you achieve anything in life by helping you to determine better ways to take control of what helps you be a more positive, confidence and happier person.

Nutrition

Nutrition introduction

Many people have previously stated, until it became quite frankly the single most misunderstood, therefore most ignored statement on Earth, *'you are what you eat'!*

That is not to say that you're a happy meal in the literal sense or indeed, a slab of tofu, but more that your body regenerates itself, on the cellular level, based on the nutrients / material that you supply it.

Some time ago there was a documentary on TV about a chap called Morgan Spurlock who ate an exclusive diet of fast food, the documentary is called 'Supersize me'.
I only know of one other person with a fixation on 'junk food', she has a serious addiction to fast food and cigars. The strange thing here is that she still had an abundance of energy, maintained a high degree of physical fitness and enjoys a vibrant positive outlook on life.

Of course, not everyone with a fast food addiction has such a positive reaction, her experience is unique to her in the same way a low carb diet might work well for someone else and a high protein diet might work great for someone else again.

Anyway, back to My Spurlock ;

'Supersize me' covered Morgans journey into the glutinous 'make it a large one' diet which lasted about a month, the ultimate conclusion being that eating too much processed fast food will make you fat, lethargic, give you bad breath and maybe even constipation, those were the good points and many people might recognise those symptoms the morning after an indulgent meal, but imagine feeling that way all the time, and worse still, accepting this as a self-imposed state of normality which advances to gastric band shopping.

The net conclusion of junk food is that it can hold the same addictive qualities as many drugs, legal and illegal.
The really bad aspect of poor diet is that it's often driven by a range personal factors, for many, when those factors are resolved, the need for junk food diminishes.

Ultimately, extended periods on junk (processed) food reliance has a serious effect under the skin, effects such as, organs giving up, hormonal responses muted and degenerative consequences for your bones and joints, it really doesn't make for good reading.

Many people might believe that a person brings those

effects on themselves, however, while the physical act of feeding is typically self-prescribed, the reasons for overeating and the over consumption of 'junk food' can be immensely complex.

It is more constructive to understand the 'why'.

This nutrition section is the most comprehensive aspect of this book, this is because what you consume is arguably the most important aspect to consider when it comes to happiness, fulfilment and being able to realise those things that will, in the longer term, enable you to attain the personal fulfilment that you rightfully deserve from life.

Many manageable well thought out minor adjustment which accumulate over time will offer the most sustainable solution to optimising your life.

The drastic single big steps aka crash diets, often result in a strong sense of denial, sacrifice and unhappiness, as such, the big step diet plans, may only result in lifelong yo-yoing in weight and wellbeing, resulting in a diminished quality of life.

Nutrition connections.

Although exercise, well-being and nutrition are in many ways equal, it could be said that good diet is the most equal of the three.
The main and most basic reason for this is that without food you will die, this fact renders everything else secondary, that's not to say that the other aspects aren't important, as you require much more than optimal nutrition alone.

Every time you consume food and drink, you're making a decision, maybe not consciously, but there's some awareness of the effect that your food choice will have on you. As such you might choose food that gives comfort when you feel low or food to energise before or after exercise and food just because you're hungry.

I'm not about to preach on about the dangers of too much sugar and fat, as your most likely already aware of those facts, besides, we all know cake and beer (to excess) are not optimal things to ingest and digest, but they taste great !

You develop a lifelong relationship with food based on your activity levels, lifestyle and sense of well-being.

Effect on Nutrition with exercise

Active people will, as a rule of thumb eat more, they primarily tend to crave carbohydrates as a ready source of energy, or protein if they are into building muscle. Of course this is simplifying matters to a point, as nutrition with exercise has many more factors requiring attention.

Here are five of the many relationships

1. Provides your body with energy
2. Reduces muscular injury.
3. Strengthens the bones.
4. Energy systems can do more and for longer.
5. Aids in recovery and re-build / renewal of the body.

Effect on Nutrition with well-being

Mental focus, happiness and confidence levels have a strong influence on your eating habits.

Here are five of the main effects;

1. You tend to eat within a regular pattern.
2. Maintains an upbeat, positive attitude.
3. Keeps you level headed.
4. The ability to retrieve information / memories.
5. You enjoy sharper mental agility.

By Mark McIntyre   35

You become what you consume

Every single one of your trillions of cells in your body has an insatiable need for balanced nutrients, what you feed your body determines everything, skin tone, nails condition, teeth, breath, energy, your general health, risk of injury, body tone, strength, immunity, sense of mental well-being and everything else determining physical and mental endurance.

Don't be made to feel guilty about your breakfast muffin, they aren't all that bad, your body loves you for eating them; The fat coats your cells, sugar is metabolised for energy and protein utilised for build, plus that happy stuff which feeds your soul and adds some joy to the day.

So, you might be thinking, hang on, he's just said that muffins are good, cake is therefore a good thing! Yes you're right, they are good, but so is organic seasonal fruit, veg and quality cuts of meat too.

As I said a moment ago, it's really important to nourish the mind and soul as well as the body in order to attain a more complete sense of fulfilment, this does occasionally come from the so called bad foods that you enjoy.

Never feel the need to endure your food or be scared

off what you enjoy; your sense of wellbeing demands it.

Good quality, balanced nutrition, means much more than merely eating what is perceived as healthy food, it is about balance, a little of what you like does zero harm, remember that what you consume affects your hormones, mental agility and can affect your entire outlook on life.

Denial diets are another way of denying happiness/

As you read through this book, you will note that I do not discourage any foods, there are very few genuinely bad foods, only poor timing.

As is often stated ;
'all things should be taken in moderation'
And *'there is a time and a place for everything'.*

So, take a read through this section, I will try and demonstrate the importance of balanced eating as opposed to rigid diet plans, which of course work for some people in the same way that a horoscope may be accurate for some.

The benefits of good nutrition

Firstly, the benefits cannot be understated, what you consume determines the quality of the building materials your body requires for regeneration.. Eat well and you will not only look great, you will feel great too.

Healthy, strong hair and nails
Hormonal response
Motivation and outlook on life
Energy production
Weight management

Quote : '*One persons food is another persons poison*'

In other words, what works for you, will not necessarily work for someone else, for this reason, diets are not a one size fits all wonder plan, even though they will try and convince you they are.

Everyone is unique; we have different backgrounds, varying heights, activity levels, jobs, home life and all the other factors which influence what, how and when you eat.

The big fat diet industry (so far)

The big fat diet industry – so far

The diet industry works on a 20/80 system
This means that 20% of people participating will see some moderate to high success, while 80% will constantly struggle to realise their slimming goals, some of the 80% leap off the diet wagon realising that fixed diets don't work for them, the remaining people stay as lifelong loyal customers to a plan that milks their misguided loyalties.
.

To those 20% I say well done, but go one step further and discover how you need never 'diet' again, while to the other 80% I say to stop blaming yourself and try and understand that it's the diet which is failing you, not you who is failing the diet.

Weight-watching and Slimslower groups, along with the diet chefs and Rosary Colon diets come across as the more popular plans, but remember, they are businesses with profit in mind and you're their sales platform. It's important to realise that they have nothing to gain from everybody seeing incredible success, you could say that seeing their entire market (you) thinning out would be terrifying for their balance sheets.

It's also worth noting that most standard diet plans are exclusively geared toward weight loss while disregarding your relationship with food.

They are fighting a single symptom while ignoring the variety of causes.

By the very nature of them, mass market diet plans simply cannot work for everyone, this is due to the one size fits all approach.
It's like a doctor giving everybody in the waiting room a standard medication even though they're all wanting to see the doctor for a range of reasons, of course the medication will work perfectly for some, but most definitely not for all.
This is also known as results by sheer luck, not by the application of knowledge.

The few that get results chant loudest.

Your body is unique in terms of how it metabolises nutrients, the types of food you like, your home and work life, the biometric patterns which are unique to you.

Not all calories are the same, and not all people process calories in the same way.

You are unique, standard doesn't quite cut it.

But you know, as previously mentioned, a diet plan will work in at least the short term for about 20% of those who partake in them.

For lifelong positive results a more measured approach may work best for you, the great thing with looking at a life-long system is that you have nothing to remember.

Expanding diet issues

As previously identified, the diet model has a particular success rate and the larger companies play on this by offering 'sin' rewards, 'guilty pleasures' and some may reward you with a 'freedom' day.

The 'diet' plan business is a business and wants to retain your custom (money), for as long as possible, they want you to become dependent, they want you to be successful, then greet you again with open arms when you fall prey to temptation again, this time you're feeling even fatter than when you originally started!

Diets often work on a system of denial, that being, denying you from the foods that you enjoy the most, although some might package their own versions of your favourite snacks and ready meals!

In general, they discourage foods not included within their programme, and their own branded product range, thus preventing you from proactively learning about foods which might work better for you.

Sometimes the diet houses may even tell you that their methods are scientifically proven, but if you're funding your own research then it stands to reason you will only publish favourable results.

Ultimately, remember that any standard model only works for about 20% of participants.

'One person's food is another person's poison'.

Yo Yo effect

Eating one day, restricting intake the next, then back to eating something healthy, then a day off to let your hair down, etc, can only cause creeping problems, the problem here is that you only notice when it becomes even more of a challenge to adopt the 'diet' yet again..

This on-off system confuses your body and consequently it can't plan the building blocks of your brand new you, this is due to it being routinely starved of valuable resources.

As a consequence, your body learns to store energy in anticipation of future food droughts. The thing is, the more droughts you have the more efficient your body learns to become, so the 2000 calories your body might require each day may come down to 1500 calories, so when you modify your intake to match the mooted 2000 calories per day for women or 2,500 per day for men, you end up consuming more than needed and as a result, your body stores the difference as fat.

RDA'a (Recommended Daily Allowances) are designed for an average that in all probably does not apply to you, unless you have 1.8 arms, 2.4 kids and drive a Mondeo.

Eating disorders

Are often caused by the by the neural pathway connections (switches) which are made throughout your life.
Many of the media driven images of success, sex and, sexuality, desirability and health are based on airbrushed models with rippling lean bodies, these are sculpted beyond any reasonably accepted norm.

You know that the images portrayed are false but still strive to attain the impossible, during the process many people become body dysmorphic, for example, believing themselves to be overweight all while eating less and less, this can ultimately lead to anorexia and psychological challenges.

The media works relentlessly to brainwash you into thinking you're worth less if you don't conform to their version of the ideal, whether it's sticking rigidly to RDA's, 5 a day or a particular brand of health food.

The word 'ideal' suggests something which is proven to be better, ie, a sexual partner may look 'ideal', as a friend they look 'ideal', as someone who should get the promotion they look 'ideal', these you would expect these to be based on demonstrable facts or at the least, personal experience.

Given an ideal is unique to you, how can anyone claim that your ideal diet is this or that, or that your ideal calorie consumption should be decided by someone who doesn't even know you exist.

The social acceptance of the media drive which fuels the 'ideal' diet industry while disregarding the ensuing eating disorders is alarming.

There are many other drivers to eating disorders such as depression caused by various personal life factors which can include bad relationships, unsupportive friends and a negative experience workplace, these issues are amplified by what you consume, i.e. the foods you eat can encourage positive hormonal responses which better equip you to deal decisively in forming solutions to enhance life decisions.

It can be argued that most 'diet' companies are set up to assist you in attaining *your* idea of perfection, or at least personal betterment, however, if the diet company you're subscribed too is not a good fit for you, they invariable stay quiet about it, instead they do all they can to suggest you must try harder to conform to their system, this amplifies the issues above.

Your unique needs are in part determined by the unique way your body processes or 'burns' the calories supplied, that being, some people have fast

metabolisms while others have slow metabolisms.
So how are people categorised then?
Everyone is averaged out, expected to fall into a pre-set category and consume a set number of calories with identical recommended daily allowances for various nutrients, currently 2500 calories per day for men and 2000 for women.

This approach is clearly unrealistic for the majority of people but this pigeon-hole system which is based purely on gender seems widely accepted and taken as gospel. I am sure you've already identified the inherent flaws in this system.

An active 6 foot woman and an inactive 5ft foot woman;

Both believe they should consume an RDA of 2000 calories.

Standard dietary information is based on this figure Points diets are often based on further simplifying RDAs

One ends up under eating, the other overeats Both could develop eating disorders

The diet business as well as media lacks understanding of the issues surrounding eating disorders, in many cases the diet industry worsens the situation by focussing heavily on the weight loss objective instead of your overall health.

People come in all shapes and sizes, have varying demands and totally different lifestyles, it is not for you to conform to a diet plan, but to choose a lifelong nutrition plan which conforms to your unique needs.

Calories make points

When asked, 'how many calories should I consume today', I often reply that I don't know. I go on to say that for me to determine how much they should be eating, with any degree of accuracy, I need to run some assessments.
Their response is that they believe it is 2000 calories a day and that they will go with that.

A few weeks later they tell me that they're having problems managing their weight...

The standardised approach of RDA of calories is tightly woven within the BMI chart (Body Mass Index).
The accepted BMI ranges do not take into account your gender, lifestyle, tradition, activity, body composition or any other factor that makes you, you! RDA and BMI are based only on averages. *You are not average.*

Another issue with calorie counting is the choice many face;
A 250 calorie glass of wine or a 300 calorie meal.

Counting calories can lead to a sense of denial, leading to feeling 'low' and could discourage physical exercise due to a disparity of demand and supply of nutrients / energy / fuel.

Calorie counting and points based diets are scientifically designed with you specifically, absolutely not in mind.

The major issue with 'fixed' diet plans

Without Sucrose, fructose, glucose, galactose, maltose, lactose and dextrose etc. the diet industry would have nothing to feed you.

Most diet products are heavy on sugars, while ironically telling you to restrict your carbohydrates! Ironic as carbohydrate and sugar are the same! Is it any wonder that many people are confused about sugar?

The other names given to sugars
Starches
Sugar (as above)
Carbohydrates
complex carbs
simple carbs
etc...

All carbohydrates are sugar (and vice versa) with different chain lengths, the longer the chain the longer it takes for your body to process, so, whole grain pasta takes longer to process than a white baguette.

Of course, the diet house rarely tell you this, they will merely inform you that they don't contain as much fat and therefore contains fewer calories, arguing this leads to weight loss.

The problem with all that sugar is that your sense of feeling hungry can be heightened, but don't worry, they have this one covered, you simply purchase their low calorie (high sugar) range of snacks to tide you over until your next high sugar low fat meal.

It is important to note that your body does require fat! Every one of the multi trillion cells requires fat, otherwise it breaks down into mush, you might recognise some the effects; brittle nails, split ends and poor complexion.

Is a sugar heavy diet plan really that bad, so long as it works?

Replacing fat with sugar can be masterstroke of criminality against your body, you will force the pancreas into overdrive, experience massive sugar highs and lows, ie, you will feel really tired and attempt to beat the tiredness by consuming more sugar to pep you up... there is the possibility of the liver being overworked, this can cause diabetes and other degenerative issues.

To be fair to the diet houses, due to consuming less energy, in theory, you could lose weight.

In many cases, the fixed diet plans now use sweeteners instead of sugar, more on that next.

Sweeteners to the rescue

AKA, saccharin, aspartame, sucralose, acesulfame, neotame, etc

Sweeteners contain even fewer calories while containing all the flavour, surely this can only be good? Well, in some ways yes it is, but it can be vastly outweighed by significant health threats, these are still being studied.

Side effects can include heightening your risks of cancer and perversely, obesity too, defying the whole reason for choosing sweeteners in the first place!

There is no nutritional benefit to artificial sweeteners and by using sweeteners and becoming dependent on them within weigh loss foods, you're discouraged to explore more natural ways to satisfy a 'sweet tooth'.

As sweeteners gain ground in the diet industry and become accepted as the norm, people are being told more by the media that the naturally occurring sugars in fruit is bad for you, but don't worry, aspartame is here to save you from the strawberry killing fields.

How sweeteners can lead to obesity;

1. Your body will demand sugar when it senses a low supply
2. Body expects sugars from certain foods
3. Brain tells you to consume something sweet
4. You reach for a low cal sweetener based snack
5. Body absorbs energy but still the sugar fix
6. Hormone system still demands sugar

Your sweetened cycle to obesity:

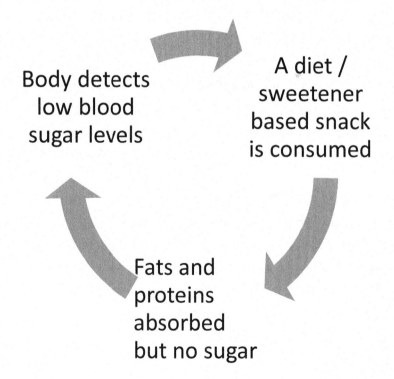

Body detects low blood sugar levels

A diet / sweetener based snack is consumed

Fats and proteins absorbed but no sugar

The body uses blood sugar levels as one of the factors to determine whether you've fed and how much energy you have, think of it as a fuel needle, if you deny your body the sugar then that needle is less likely to register that you have eaten according to what your body actually needed.
(The entire process is more complex than this in actuality).

The net result is that the sweetener cycle can lead to weight gain, this is due to consuming everything but what your body wanted in the first place, if you listened and consumed something naturally sweet, you will have only taken in say 150 calories instead of 400 calories, but by trying to force your body to accept an alternative by snacking frantically on the too good to be true products and slimmer slower product, you may be achieving the exact opposite of what the diet plan suggests you should experience

Think of it as telling your partner to go out and buy a bag of sugar, they come back with tea, coffee and biscuits, but no sugar, you send them out again and this time they buy socks and a pineapple, in-fact, every time to send them out to buy sugar, they disappoint by not purchasing it.

You just end up with a lot of shopping to pack away.

Remember that reducing sugars and refined sugar in particular can be a great thing to do for medical reasons including weight control. Sweeteners can be a Trojan horse to obesity. Try to keep it natural as much as you're able.

Fat lot of good

Fats are absolutely vital for full human function, and here is a brief explanation of why;

The body is composed of trillions of cells, each of these cells can break down very quickly if not protected by it's membrane which is essentially a thin layer fat, every cell requires this to protect its form and function.

It may help to imagine a cell as being similar to a cube of sugar, if it gets wet then its structural integrity suffers, ie it dissolves.
But if you wrap that cube of sugar in a protective film (ie fat) and pour water on it then it retains its form.
And that explains the job of fat on a very basic level.

So, think about your skin, if those cells which make up your skin are not properly protected due to being on a fat (severely) restrictive diet, then over time you're highly likely to end up with poor skin, of course this is merely the visual indicator of your body being denied essential nutrients, but the effects run further than the superficial on the surface,

Your immune system could suffer greatly over time and you may also experience circulatory issues amongst a vast array of physiological complications, this could promote hormonal imbalances that drive feelings of negativity.

The body is unable to produce some of its own fats, these are known as Essential Fatty Acids, aka omega 3 and 6, these EFA's enhance body function, including the central nervous system and helps with many issues surrounding well-being.

Omega 3 – fish oils, eggs, nuts and seeds

Omega 6 – Plant oils then Eggs, seeds, nuts, dairy, meat

Unsaturated : Think olive oil, avocado, nuts and vegetable oils... Unsaturated fats have slightly fewer calories than their saturated counterpart, however the trade off is that many sources of food actually contain saturated and unsaturated fats.

Monounsaturated : These foods can help to reduce LDL (Low density lipoproteins) and increase HDL (High density lipoproteins) i.e., they reduce cholesterol, foods included are, grape seed oil, sesame oil, whole grain wheat, oatmeal, sunflower oil, avocado

Saturated: Generally from animal sources, these fats are highly stable at high temperatures and therefore lend themselves to be used within frying foods... Sources include dairy and animal however, there are alternatives to animal fats in the form of cottonseed oil, palm and coconut oil.

Trans: The only fat that the body does not require, trans fats are the by product of poor cooking practice, that is using unstable oils to cook at high temperatures and the practice of hydrogenation of oils and fats, a process used extensively to keep pre-packed meals stable (including many diet meals), also within some margarines, including the 'light' versions. Trans-fats are widely considered as being carcinogenic.

I previously mentioned fats being stripped from diet foods in favour of sugar or sweeteners and the problems associated with that process. Are you starting to view balance as being a better option yet?

Pointing to a better way the future?

Pointing to a better way – The future?

First of all, if your eating plan is working brilliantly for you and you enjoy it, then for the most part, stick with it, however, it's good to try new things and to experiment a little, this builds up your knowledge and overall enjoyment of food, but more critically (perhaps), your understanding of food and how it acts specifically within your body...

This section is all about presenting you with alternative ideas which promotes eating in a way to maximise your feel good vibe, balance your hormonal response and give you the freedom to enjoy the foods you really enjoy, while keeping your body and mind in balance.

So, feel healthy, energetic, experience all the great flavours that the world has to offer you and feel great foodie satisfaction.

Shun the diet plan

It's a tough thing to do, after all, you're friends use them, you feel bad for leaving a group and you quite enjoy the weigh-in competition.

Big house diet plans are all the more difficult to shake off because they're incredibly addictive too, not only in terms of the sugar, but with the promises that they make...

They utilise the carrot and stick approach in its most devastatingly efficient manner;

1. They dangle the carrot (make the promise).
2. You're identified with faults and issues
3. You end up buying into their branded foods
4. This results in higher sugar and sweetener uptake
5. If you lose a pound it is down to the diet
6. If you gain a pound it's your fault
7. Peer pressure to accept guilt if it doesn't work for you

That cycle can last for years, in part, due to going to the 'weigh ins' as moral support for a friend. You realise it works for them and this heightens your sense of personal failure and the ensuing downward spiral of personal depreciation and guilt which can have long lasting emotional and physical challenges.

By Mark McIntyre   70

The diet house business is there to make a profit, while they do work brilliantly for 20% of their customers in the mid to longer term, the remaining 80% blame themselves when the diet fails to work, this is the business model and encourages the following sentiment which bizarrely helps them retain the very people that their plan is a poor fit for;

'if the 20% can do it then I must be doing something wrong'

The diet house is apparently blameless, but you're now beginning to realise that this is far from the truth and understanding this will hopefully make you feel 'normal'.

Obviously if you're the 20% then a huge thumbs up to you, and continue as you are, but it might be worth trying some of the other bits of advice in the book and paying more focus to exercise and the factors effecting your well-being, to heighten your journey to greater happiness and positivity.

Strategic eating

You love your treats and under many diet plans you're allowed them occasionally, but they are referred to as sins, what about a system where you're not made to feel guilty about enjoying the foods that make you happier?

Of course, moderation is key, so try not to interpret this as me saying you should feast upon every pizza place in town, followed by visiting every pub to wash down said pizza with gallons of booze.... I really am not about to suggest this as the credible and healthy way to go, sorry about that.

The principle behind strategic eating is to consume the higher energy foods earlier in the day. For this I will use the favourite snack / treat consumed by most people. Chocolate.

Instead of eating chocolate in the evening with your bottle of wine, while watching sport on TV, it's better to consume the chocolate earlier in the day, before 3pm is ideal, but only if you were to eat this types of treat anyway.
The main reason for this is that you give your body more of a chance of burning through the energy that you've consumed

Of course there are many health benefits to chocolate, but if you enjoy chocolate try and go for a higher quality, higher cocoa content, i.e., dark chocolate, from this many enjoy the happy vibe, the tryptophan and serotonin release being a part of this, the caffeine / stimulant aspect being another, great as a sweet tooth craving satisfier prior to a workout....

Chocolate can have you feeling great, alert and ready for anything, best of all, instead of using it as a naughty sin based treat, you can, through strategic eating, enjoy it completely guilt free and to great benefit.

Does this suit you better?

Nutrition plays such an important role in the sense of wellbeing, it drives motivation and controls your ability for physical exertion, i.e., exercise.
Nutrition has been hijacked by the slim groups who don't care about anything other than losing weight.
A real lie to life!

But what about those who need to increase weight?

Strategic eating can lend itself to the image of an army general at the breakfast table talking of pincer movements while moving the condiments like chess pieces, but in reality the strategic eating method is so well known that it has its own quote.

By Mark McIntyre

'Breakfast like a king, lunch like a prince, dine like a pauper'

Combine strategic eating with your physical exercise routine and you have the ideal solution, for 20% of you anyway.

Strategic eating is great to enhance your overall sense of wellbeing, you're not tied to targets, points, quotas, sins, good days, bad days, green or red, or any other control mechanism.

It is sustainable for life, everyone in your household can benefit with very little adjustment and you can directly benefit from balanced nutrition, maintained energy, elevated mental wellbeing, these elements conspire to greater positivity which encourages more intense exercise, whether this is longer walks with the dog, attending the gym or whatever suits..

A Positively Healthier Lifestyle

Sympathetic in demand

You know when you're hungry and when you're not, but most of us tend to eat within a particular pattern as a matter of routine whether or not that meal is required, not only that but we tend to eat the same volumes of food at the same times of the day regardless of whether you need that for energy purposes..

Eating in harmony with what your body demands can be a great system, but it does take some time and effort to retrain yourself into eating in this way.

The only real problem with following this approach is the tendency of sympathetic eaters to consume convenience foods on demand instead of freshly prepared meals.

With this method, the ability and will to plan your healthier meals and snacks in advance is critical, you should factor into your meals enjoyment and balance.

Once you've trained yourself you may find this system of eating to be quite intuitive, it's a self-checking system that's naturally balances nutrition consumption. That being, over time you learn to eat in a way that is in harmony with your bodies' energy requirements.

If your lifestyle is generally sedate then don't be too shocked if you occasionally eat a little less, if you have a busy day then your body may demand more food as a consequence.

This system can be hugely rewarding when combined with a clearer idea of the best foods for you and an improved sense of portion control.

This system is difficult to beat, mostly because there's nothing to think about and you're not denied any of the foods you enjoy.

Portion Control

Getting a good portion can sound exciting and as we all know, bigger is better... but it could be time to question that outlook.

The elephant in every household is that almost everybody eats too much, we use our eyes to judge the value of food based on quantity, in fact, quantity might be the goal of many meals, stack it high, fence it in, pile it on, bigger plates and having to clear your plate are often the norm.

The continuing trend is that portion sizes are ever increasing, a typical fast food meal will contain half the energy a grown man requires for an entire day, even pre-packaged diet meals often provide portion sizes which are 30-50 percent too big, as they are after all, designed for the mystical average person.

But don't fear, this is where you get to fight back and take control in a number of really easy to adopt methods, so try some of them and see how you get on.

Often, the most effective solution is the simplest one.

A healthy handful

Your hands are generally in proportion to your body, you can therefore use them to determine portions for types of food, for example;

Meat = size and thickness of your palm
Pasta = 2 handfuls
Rice = 1 handful
Oats = 1 handful

This continues for everything else that you would consume, it can be trial and error but once you've determined the number of handfuls per food item, then you know you're eating proportionally, that being, you are consuming volumes of food which are in tune with your unique requirements. Handy that!

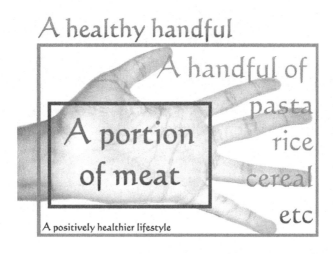

A healthy handful

A handful of pasta rice cereal etc

A portion of meat

A positively healthier lifestyle

Count the calories

To effectively count calories you have to be able to deconstruct your meals, that is, separate the carbs, fats, protein and even the alcohol, and then tot up the numbers.

The benefit of doing this is that you know precisely what you're eating, the drawback is that it takes discipline to measure, weigh and analyse every meal, though you might enjoy this aspect as it gives you absolute control.

The following are based on 1 gram of each category

Carbs	= 4 calories
Protein	= 4 calories
Fat	= 9 calories
Alcohol	= 7.5 calories (In basic terms)

Use this method to add up the calorific values given on many pre-packed meals (included diet meals) instead of taking for granted the numbers they provide as their 'at a glance' systems, you might be surprised how much their numbers are understated.

Smaller plates

We're usually highly visual when it comes to the appreciation of what we are about to consume, if you have a huge plate with a single portion of food then you're likely to feel dissatisfied and this can lead to you snacking later on or simply piling more food on your massive plate right now.

By using smaller plates you don't have to count, measure or chant. On a smaller plate a single portion suddenly looks about right and can lead to you feeling more satisfied before and after eating, you will find that you snack less too.

How smaller feeels bigger

Hungry   Full

Each plate has the same volume of food!

A positively healthier lifestyle

Padding

If you can't stand the thought of calorie counting, using your hands, measuring, weighing and even the thought of using smaller plates leaves you feeling cold, then padding might work for you.

Padding works by adding more veg and even fruit to your meals, try to keep the fruit and veg as close to raw as possible and remember to eat the skins where it is typically conventional to do so, this adds fibre which contains no useable energy but it helps you feel fuller.

The fibre also aids in your digestive process, so a double win.

Pre-Padding can also include drinking a glass of water just before you start eating.

These tricks allow you to consume what you enjoy and naturally control the energy rich portions of your meals.

Take your time

I realise that it might seem a bit odd, but our bodies can be a little slow on the uptake, even though the saliva is flowing, the pupils dilated and the heart races a bit on seeing your favourite meal, the digestive system only starts to respond a few minutes after eating, often mooted as a 20 minute delay.

Eating slowly is the answer, this gives your body time to appreciate the fact that you're eating and goes some way to help prevent overeating. By eating slowly, you give the 'full sensors' time to register when you've had enough.

So enjoy your food, appreciate it, make it a social occasion and stop eating when full.

It is okay to not clear your plate.

On a cruise without booze

Alcohol makes many people feel relaxed, there is so much variety that we can all identify a drink we enjoy with a meal, whether it's a refreshing glass of Pinot with lunch on a summers day, or a bottle of Indian beer with your curry...

The thing is, that cold liquid refreshment can come at a price on your weight management..

Imagine that you've been saving points or counting calories, the glass of wine is a welcome break and keeps you comfortably within the confines of your diet plan, it might be a sin but it's only a glass of wine and a sneaky second perhaps, how can this make any difference?

When you eat a meal with a glass of wine, or any other alcoholic drink for that matter, the body will think to itself, 'yeah, liking the food but hang on, what's this?' Your body detects the poison (alcohol) and becomes focussed only on the alcohol and getting it out of your system, the quickest way is to try and convert the alcohol into energy, unfortunately, during this process you're body disregards the energy in the meal which you just consumed, in short, that meal is stored as fat with the possibility of being dealt with at a later date.

If you can't live without your favourite tipple then consume it at least a couple of hours either side of eating, this gives your body a fighting chance of processing the alcohol in the usual manner with fewer calories to store.

The other concern with alcohol is that it can become highly addictive and destructive to your body, but also to your sense of well-being through destabilising the hormonal system and diminishing mental focus.

This is not a dink aware funded publication, however, do try to keep within the guidelines (yes, for the average person).

14 units for women per week
21 units for men per week.

Take in no more than 3 units in any one day
Try and take 2 or more days a week without any alcohol consumption at all.

There is a lot to being 'drink aware', but also be aware that your body will always prioritise the processing of alcohol at great detriment to the food you consumed with it.

In summery

It's generally modest to excessive alcohol consumption with meals that contributes more to the mechanics of gaining weight than the actual food consumed.

That cheeky tipple with a meal is the Trojan horse which makes weight control so challenging for many.

If you are a regular drinker (with meals and snacks) then as a personal experiment, try not drinking alcoholic beverages for two weeks.

Exercise

Exercise introduction

Exercise is something that many people consider to be as pleasant as a wisdom tooth extraction, but that's possibly down to the way the media as well as the fitness industry (in general) sells the notion and the worth of exercise.

It can get you in a sweat just thinking about it, unfortunately for some, that being a cold sweat, this is because there's a lot to terrify most people, from the lycra image to the never ending mirrored reflections of what you perceive as being your inferior body shape compared to the posters etc.

Then there are the gym instructors who all seem to have the perfect body, rippling 6 packs and buns of steel, blimey, they even have perfect teeth and hair too...

Exercise and fitness are generally promoted as exclusively purchased from the gym, the Mecca of airbrushed body perfection. The fitness industry prioritises the chiselled physical ideals instead of pushing the ideal of function and mobility. This message is reflected on their websites and posters in the gym, extremely toned female and body builder male forms.

Put this to the test and check the posters in the gym which advertise classes or themselves.

Where are the regular looking people?

Fortunately, the gym is not the exclusive provider of a physically active and fitter lifestyle, you can choose a deeper understanding the alternatives and of the enhanced benefits to your health, well-being and the enrichment of life from physical activity on your terms from alternative sources.

Exercise can be what you choose to make it, whether it's a brisk coastal walk or indeed, embracing every fitness class you can imagine.

Like nutrition, the choice of exercise is a personal one, whatever you choose to do, there must be the genuine interest factor to keep you going, more importantly though, you should be doing it for you, not pushed into it from external sources, i.e. the media pushing you to conform to their concept of fit and healthy.

If you're feeling quite tentative about taking that first step into a more active lifestyle, then seeking guidance from a fitness professional is often a great way to start, of course you can exercise with a friend or join some activity groups, such as walking, skydiving or Latin dance etc, this allows you to break into a more active lifestyle on your own terms, while having fun, thus enjoying it more and sticking at it.

By Mark McIntyre   91

Exercise connections

Exercise is tremendously important for your body and mind.

It makes you feel 'alive'.
Highly motivational.
Enhances mental focus.
Strengthens the body.
Enhances your immune system.
Improves posture.
Enhances confidence.
Boosts self-belief.
Encourages competition.
Regulates hunger better.
Improves the digestive process.
Encourages healthier eating.
etc.

Basically, exercise and physical activity is what our bodies are made for, our bodies are finely tuned to perform a vast range of movements with grace and power, strength and agility.
Through exercise we enhance our hormonal responses and overall state of well-being.

Exercise and Nutrition

The link between exercise and nutrition is obviously a very strong one; however, there are many ways in which exercise has a major impact on the foods you choose to consume.
Here are 5 examples;

1. You 'burn' more calories consumed
2. You tend to link certain foods with physical performance
3. You can get away with eating more of what you enjoy
4. Food knowledge increases
5. Consume less alcohol

Exercise and well-being

Unsurprisingly, the well-being of those people who exercise tends to be greater than for those who don't, the reasons are many and diverse, but here are 5 of them ;

1. The happy vibe (serotonin)
2. Heightened sense of achievement.
3. Allows you to de-stress (offload negative emotions)
4. It can be extremely sociable
5. Encourages positive competition and self belief

Consequences of physical lethargy

Doing nothing is the riskiest thing you can do, or not. Lethargy breeds more lethargy, laziness and procrastination.

Given that the benefits of exercise are so many and proven, why do we seem predisposed to do as little as possible? I think a little explanation is required to help you understand.

Our bodies are lazy, when I say lazy, I mean really lazy, they will do whatever is necessary to convince you that sitting down on a comfy sofa eating burgers is a heroic thing to do. Worse than that, your body will get you hooked on lethargy thanks to serotonin releases to make you feel good about it, even worse is the sense of anxiety when you decide to break the cycle. Serotonin is often more desirable.

Lethargy is a survival mechanism, it saves our bodies from wasting energy as it also saves us from excessive wear and tear on the joints and muscles etc.
Why expend energy for no apparent useful purpose?
What if there is a food drought round the corner?
What if you need that energy for a fight or flight reflex later? So over time, the hormonal system developed incentives and rewards for lethargy.

Of course that hormonal reward response came about when food was scarce and a lot of energy was naturally expended in obtaining food in the first place, in short, when sourcing food ran greater risk to your physical wellbeing than a shopping trip to the supermarket today.
This creates a modern day challenge

That reward system which evolved over time is no, in many ways, defunct in the modern age of plenty.

Your body is the pinnacle of evolution, a dynamic, versatile form which allows a vast range of movement patterns, agility, power and control. To maintain these properties your body must be active, stimulated and challenged, mixed physical activity achieves this.
Going back to the serotonin release, it is fortunate that exercise also encourages it, you just have to break the cycle.

If you adopt the Neanderthal approach , i.e., lethargy 90% of the time and action 10% of the time, then your long term outlook might look like this;

Significantly Increased or decreased blood pressure
Coronary heart disease
Muscular wastage leading to poor posture
Brittle bones and frequent muscle strains
Obesity leading to psychological challenges
By Mark McIntyre   95

Worth the time and energy

It can be said that exercise is time consuming and the benefits are often visually difficult to identify, especially when standing on the scales or looking in the mirror.

Identifying daily micro changes is borderline impossible and can only make you feel despondent, this is what may lead many people to you believing that they're wasting their time.

You can save yourself from this by not prodding, poking measuring and analysing too often, instead think about how you actually feel about your progress and activities.

You might drive to the gym or fitness class but once there you work at a sub-optimal level, performing a range of exercises that might not appropriate for your personal needs, of course there are also the distractions, such as TV screens chit chat.

Three months worth of watching TV will, unsurprisingly lead to underwhelming results.

You get out what you put in, so make sure that what you put in is appropriate in the first place.

With regard to structured physical exercise, it is a dirty sweaty business where the idea is to expend energy, heat and sweat, ultimately feeling a sense of achievement.
Do this for about Three hours per week and you will feel significant changes to your body and mindset.

For those wanting to be more active while not consciously sacrificing too much time, or indeed for those people for whom the gym and classes hold nothing but fear, then the following routine activities could be of tremendous benefit;

Gardening, hiking, taking the stairs instead of the lift, walking briskly, cycling to work etc are worthy things to do and can be absorbed into your everyday life without even thinking about it, the cumulative effect can offer many of the benefits of structured exercise.

Exercise is merely physical activity with purpose.

With this purposeful activity comes a rush of endorphins, a welcome surge of the feel good vibe, a hormonal reward of a job well done, a pick up on mental focus, personal determination, self belief and confidence.

So yes, physical exercise and physical activity is worth the time and effort.

By Mark McIntyre

In the net! Focussing on goals

Goals, targets, tick boxes, the bigger picture, competition, massive challenges and all the other ways to suggest a drastic transformation in terms of improved body shape, as that's what the fitness business trades on, seems to be the high pressure norm.
The thing is, do you really need to be reminded every 5 minutes of what your goal is? This could be tantamount to viewing your present self as substandard, is that motivational for everyone?

Some people thrive on goal setting and then focus with single minded determination on that goal until they have achieved it... but what everyone else?

If goal setting works for you then great news..

For those wanting more while not feeling intimidated by the culture of chasing the curve, a better way ahead might include exercising for the enjoyment of it, difficult to envisage if you believe 'enjoyment' and 'exercise' go together like lamb gravy and cheesecake.

The main factors to consider when setting goals;

How will you benefit from attaining the goal
Have you planned a route to your goal
What is your fall back option due to injury
What happens after you achieve your goal
Who is the goal for?
Why those specific goals?

The following sub parts to this chapter cover the main points above.

Goals can be a reminder of the current

Goal setting for many can lead onto a cycle of self doubt and encourage a negative frame of mind, this is due to the constant self-judgement of the current self image to the goal self-image.

The comparisons you might make are often based on the relentless images of the media idea of perfection, comparing yourself against other people and the blown up images on the gym posters, in the magazines and on TV of what you should be looking to physically attain.

Achieving you goal can take a long time, but many people expect instant results.

The net result, for many, can often be a loss of interest in your pursuit of being fitter and happier, due to the unrealistic expectation you have formed from the messages of dropping dress sizes in 28 days or look like a Spartan in month.

It is the gym and the media that has miss-sold this image to you.

Being more active for fun can often lead to the most impressive transformation, physically and mentally.

Who is the goal for?

This is a tricky one, when people are asked they quite often don't really know why they've set a particular goal, you might say that you want to be fitter so you look and feel better in your clothes, while other people may say it's to look good on the beach, the crucial thing here is that fitness and body shape are two entirely different things.

Focussing on body shape as the goal can lead to temporary outlook to fitness, after all if all you want is to look toned on the beach while on holiday, then what drives you to continue your fitness after your holiday?

Whoever the goal is for, it is often based on body shape or losing weight, this can lead onto a range well-being issues which include eating disorders and body dysmorphia.

As a personal mental exercise; when considering the reasons for being healthier, completely disregard anything that is based on body-weight alone.

The best goal to have is to be fitter through fun activities, body shape will come as a happy side effect of this.

Why those goals

Sometimes you set the goal based on what other people tell you, or on how you perceive the world expects you to look.
It's astonishing how marketing campaigns have a subtle yet decisive influence on how you form your fitness goals.

The fear of loss

Do you feel that your partner might look for a 'better model'

The promise of Sex

Physical fitness has become incredibly sexualised, even so far as professional sports arenas. An athlete won't be judged on their performance, but on whether the commentator would want to sleep with them due to their six pack or nice figure !

If you enhance your physical form, then you too might attracts sexual partner.

The illusion of success

The media joins physical fitness with happy successful people, likewise, larger or unfit people are twinned with failure or the underdog.

Be aware of the tricks played that try to form your goals and remember that the main goal should be on you being happier and fitter for the life you lead.

No pain no gain

There are many remnants from the 1970's 'Pumping Iron' genre that persist today despite the huge advances in the field of sports research which tell us that pain is bad, as if you really needed me to remind you of that.

After millions of years of physical faux pas resulting in broken bones, detached limbs and ripped muscle etc, we evolved a complex network of pain receptors, this setup informs the brain when you've just performed a dangerous physical action.

Here's the pain reflex ;

You perform a movement that is potential dangerous
Brain orders a taser shot to the leg
Leg tells brain, 'Sorry, I overstrained'
Brain transmits a message back to the leg,
'you've been warned, now be careful'
Leg responds with 'good idea' and stops the
movement.
You remember this lesson and don't overstrain again.

That's how it should work, but thanks to all the stupid fitness slogans since the 1970's, we have started to think we're somehow able to defy millions of years of evolution.

Are you still convinced that 'no pain no gain' makes sense, okay, here's an analogy ;

Would you walk up to a police officer and ask them taser you? If you say yes, then you need help!

If like most people you say, 'of course not', then you should now disregard the 'no pain no gain' philosophy to exercise.

If you're injured or feel pain then stop, this is really important, giving your body time to recover and repair as required is much better in the long term.

It only takes one month to lose three months of fitness progress! So, even when injured, stay mobile, choose activities without causing undue stress on the injured area, a sore leg does not impede the ability to perform core exercise, a sore thumb does not prevent you from running. Keep to prevent slipping into lethargy mode.

Listen to your body, you understand it better than anyone.

Gym-haters paradise

Many people and maybe you too, feel the gym is about as welcoming as Christmas is to a turkey (if it knew). Maybe you firmly believe the entire concept of driving to the gym to jog on the spot on a treadmill, surrounded by vanity and judgement is not particularly appealing.

At this point it must be said that it you like the gym, then carry on with it, after all, this is your focal point and if it's working out for you then that's sweet, however, it can be beneficial to explore other things too. Remember that everyone has different tastes.

As Rita Mae Brown stated in her book Sudden Death. "Insanity is doing the same thing over and over again but expecting different results."

So, if you want to feel fitter or take your fitness to the next level then do something different, by the way, most people attribute that quote to Einstein, you're already learning something new...

Personal motivation can be tough, especially when you feel that you *have* to do something in order to fit in, you will find that to feel motivated through sweating and raised heart rate you must embark on something offering the excitement of the 'F' word, yes, fun!

By Mark McIntyre   106

You may be thinking that to lead an active and healthier lifestyle means having to set aside time to go to the gym, or hire the services of a personal trainer, well, this isn't always the case thankfully.

I say thankfully because even though many gym based personal trainers are great at counting, with some of the better ones managing to count to ten during every single exercise that you perform in some pseudo motivational manner, the novelty soon loses its value, ultimately it can become distracting at best.
The cheesy grin and the nonstop clichés serving as motivational sound-bites cease to inspire.

Okay gym-hater, have I got you onside yet?
Here we go with some of the main the alternatives which still provide similar experiences to the gym, but without the mirrors, baby oil and people with noisy headphones.

Here are four suggestions to help;
Community centre
Outdoor group fitness
Workout videos / home gym
Going for a run

Community centres

These places can be pure gold, obviously you have to wade through the usual classes to get to the ones you like the sound of and dare I say it, get excited about!

Community centres tend to offer the exercise classes that the gyms don't consider to be 'of the moment', what this means is that all the favourites, are there!

Many community centres have classes for new mums, the elderly or those with mobility issues as well as the Latin dance themed classes in amongst the kettle-bell sessions too, presented by genuinely skilled and passionate instructors.

The community centre becomes your workout zone and social zone too, the best bit is that after your workout there's usually a coffee morning with cake - winner!

Outdoor group fitness

There are many groups offering outdoor fitness classes, prominent classes tend to be bootcamps, they typically have a work hard play hard ethos.

Exercising in the outdoors is really good for you, it can be extremely social and you don't have to wear the latest and most expensive training kit, a set of sweats and good trainers make you good to go.

So, cost effective fitness results, tons of calories burnt and stacks of fresh air in a rather sociable environment too.

Great if you demand stacks of encouragement, heightened personal confidence levels and elevated positivity overall.

Workout videos and home gyms etc

Many people absolutely thrive on these, after-all, you can download a workout from YouTube for free and do them at home or anywhere else that you fancy, including the bus, train or frozen food section of the grocery store should the need take you.

Your mobile phone can now be your fitness instructor and show you how to better use your weights, the pilates machine or your cross trainer, why go to the gym when it's all in the palm of your hand!

With workout videos and the home gym you have the option to involve your friends or do it alone, there's loads of variety available for free, meaning you can change workouts every month and you don't have to fit in with a group etc.

Workout videos do require a high degree of self-motivation and the ability to not stop mid-way when the phone rings etc.

Going for a run

Running is one of the most accessible forms of fitness out there, you can do it at anytime and you can control the rate of work and the rate of your progress.

You will also find that the world is freely accessible 24/7, this means you can benefit from the total freedom to exercise when and where you choose.

Of course, you can also join running clubs and take part in competition; every town has a running club.

Running to a time or distance is a great way to self motivate, the encouragement of clubs can really drive you on and enhance your confidence too, you might find it pleasantly addictive.

It doesn't seem to be working out

The whole thought of subscribing to a gym or a fitness class or indeed making any specific effort to take part in sports or workouts in any shape or form might be as welcome to you as a snake on your plane!

If you're happy with your workouts then it's still worth reading this bit just so you can appreciate all the extra activity you're doing, without having classed it as exercise...

So, let's go on the journey that demonstrates that you're a secretive fitness fanatic, without realising it;

Sex   *150 calories per hour*
Hard as it is to believe, sex burns calories, it can help tone your body, enhance shape and it's fun
(so I'm lead to believe)

Gardening   *250 calories per hour*
Maintaining the garden is demanding, enhances flexibility, mobility, stability and enhances muscular endurance - brilliant for all over toning.

Shopping   *300 calories per hour*
Bags of; walking, lifting, squatting, sitting, brisk walks, stairs, dragging, pushing, moving, lowering etc.
This can be a highly energetic activity.

Housework *250 calories per hour*
Hoovering sucks, but it works your shoulders, back, legs, there is lifting, pushing and pulling, flexibility and stability as you stand on one leg to reach a corner etc...

Looking after the kids *300 calories per hour*
Groaning pains of running after them, lifting, spinning, walking, jumping, cooking, cleaning after them, often entertaining and exhausting!

Going to work *200 calories per hour*
If your job is physically demanding job or requires *.more mental focus* then you're burning tons of energy via the central nervous system or the muscles.

So, if you're regularly doing 3 or more of the above activities then this can equate to more exercise than most gym bunnies do in a week without even realising it! Do you now feel superior? Well done!

Doing many daily activities with purpose has many benefits, i.e., the sense of completing a job or enjoying the results of fruits of your labour etc can lead to a positive state of mind, this is very similar to that experienced by a winning athlete.

Too late to motivate?

Lacking motivation to exercise or do physical activity often stems from fear of looking silly, failing, or even the fear of being judged by others.

You might have convinced yourself that trying to exercise is futile, thus killing your motivation.

It is possible that you've hit the stage where you try dissuading others from embarking on exercise by verbalising to them, the very comments that you dread hearing about yourself.

Thankfully there are groups which can help you, particularly if you've suffered a mental or physical trauma which may subsequently formed barriers to your participation in physical activity.

Even with these groups, it has to start with you making a leap of faith, you might be finding this bit quite tough.

It's never too late to embrace a more positive approach to physical activity; the smallest step is still a step.

Break the cycle

By Mark McIntyre

The very first thing to do to encourage self motivation is absolutely anything, no matter how minor it may seem.

So today, get up five minutes earlier or eat fish instead of steak, read a different magazine etc, the idea is to break your regular cycle, this encourages you to believe that the usual routine can be improved and possibly changed entirely over the longer term to better yourself, of course this starts with a single first step, it is this first step which is the hardest, do this and anything is possible.

Once you start breaking the cycle, do more, one small step at a time until you feel confident enough to make changes that positively effect on your physical well-being.

You could start by going for a walk in the park
That walk becomes a brisk walk
That is then complemented by adapting what you eat
You start to feel more upbeat
You can run for a minute, then 5 then 10 etc,
Running times and distance increasing each week
Your diet changes a bit more, you're feeling quite buzzy

We can fast forward and in twelve months you have, under your own steam and self motivation managed to attain the level where you're exercising for an hour at a time, you eat well but still enjoy your favourite foods, your weight is under control and you enjoy greater energy and confidence. People now tell you that you're their inspiration, WOW!

This happened by making a single modest change, seemingly unrelated to what you ultimately achieved.

The thing is, we do become set in our ways, the minds will tell the body what to do and our bodies mould themselves to the environment that we make for it, but this can be reversed or enhanced, simply by deciding to do something else.

On a cellular level, this time in 13 months you're 100% brand new, that is every single cell in your body, your, heart, your bones, your eyes, brain, and toes, everything is new... you're effectively an entirely different person.

If you do nothing then in 13 months you will be a facsimile of who you are right now, do something different and the knock on effect means you effectively become a different person.

If a stranger asked you if they could run a half marathon in a year, you would likely encourage them, oddly you might, at the same time you convince yourself that you can't do it because of your current abilities.

You will likely make mistakes, but those mistakes are your stepping stones to the success as you see it... and this leads us nicely to the next chapter.

Well-being

Well-being introduction

Your confidence, self belief and overall mental well-being is under relentless assault on multiple fronts, it's a war of the senses, the battle of wills and the relentless struggle to stay on top, no matter what.

Staying positive could involve you;
Doing good deeds
Following a religion
Making affirmations in the mirror, 'I am successful', or 'I will be rich', even, 'I am loved'.

Mental well-being is difficult to measure in conventional terms, thus typically dismissed by society as a serious issue; this can leave many people feeling alone.
The irony with this sense of isolation is that everybody is affected, in varying shades of grey at some stage in life.

It can be argued that the serious disparity between physical and mental treatment is that we base value and experience on what we can see, touch, feel and smell, not how we 'feel' emotionally.

This is effectively a state of physical/emotional apartheid; those with physical trauma receive a warm welcome while those with emotional trauma are left out in the cold.

It's really unfortunate that in the modern era there is still a cruel disparity between the physical and emotional trauma that so many people face. Many people, at some stage in life might require an injection of positivity and confidence to enhance their sense of well-being just as some may need a pain injection and bandages to tend to a broken bone.

Mental well-being experiences:

You may be prescribed a 'mental balancing' drug.
Drug provided on a recurring basis (to save future visits)
You feel like you're not taken seriously
Employers fail to make allowances
Families and friends fail to understand
Many people just tell you to 'get over it' or 'soldier on'

Broken leg

Doctor has the leg x-rayed, treated and cast etc
Follow up treatment may include physiotherapy
You feel like you've been treated like a god
Employers may provide sick leave or flexible working hours
Friends and family proactively assist you
Strangers empathise with your story and want to help you.

By Mark McIntyre   125

There are three main routes to improve a negative state of wellbeing, if you're currently on a course of treatment then do not suddenly stop or change, always seek the advice from your practitioner or doctor.

Prescribed Drugs
Counselling
Self Help

Prescribed drugs

These offer a short term passive remedy to help you come to terms with your emotional trauma.

If you're prescribed these drugs then do keep taking them, at the same time, try to adopt some small changes to your life, in short, a controlled pathway that ensures a more positive direction as you gradually remove the dependency of the drugs that you're prescribed. .

The drugs you may have prescribed to you are tasked with neutralising emotions, they effectively help prevent the very low feelings but your moments of elation could be sacrificed as a consequence.

You're effectively set on an even keel.

Remember that these drugs are a short term measure, so do see your doctor to be weaned off in partnership with counselling.

Counselling

This tends to offer the highest degree of help, the fact that someone will listen to you without judging you is often enough to help.

Unfortunately, even in this age, there seems to be a stigma attached to counselling, it can also be viewed as being rather expensive and puts many people off a course of treatment which is proven to be extremely effective.

If you needed a heart transplant, would the cost put you off? Your sense of well-being should be treated on equal terms.

Your state of mental well-being is extremely important. It the thing that defines you, encourages you, fuels your ambitions and your determination, wellbeing has you making better decisions, winning friends, it encourages exercise and better diet.

Positive well-being is critical.

If you're not seeking therapy / counselling while feeling 'low', then this is one thing you can change today.
If your GP offers you drugs, ask for counselling instead or in addition to the drugs.

Helping yourself

The act of finding a way to self-help can hand back to you the sense of control, if you're under medication or counselling then by working in parallel to their advice, you can help yourself to rebuild your positivity and enhanced well-being, this can help you feel more empowered and involved within your personal journey.

Of course, self-help can work out brilliantly;
What you do and how you achieve it depends on your personal situation.

The very act of identifying that you could benefit from enhancing and improving your confidence and positivity (for whatever the reason) is the most major aspect of self-help.

Only once it becomes a known known can you act in the most progressive and constructive manner.

Connections

A positive state of wellbeing is extremely important, your personal belief of being able to achieve anything and your confidence in varied situations can help other people feel great.

Wellbeing affects your approach to nutrition

Extensive research shows that food plays a major role in determining your mental well-being and outlook. For example, some of the many E-numbers, additives and preservatives have been shown to trigger or amplify adverse emotional problems, while whole foods can enhance them.
Some foods can be highly addictive; unfortunately these tend to be the junk foods and oddly, some diet foods too. After the happy vibe they can result in adverse wellbeing issues.

Five positive effects of positive wellbeing on nutrition;

1. Increases your chances of eating more healthily
2. Reduces the possibility comfort eating and 'food rewards'
3. You eat in moderation
4. Your food choices become optimal for you
5. You don't feel guilty about treats

Wellbeing effects whether or how you exercise

Your sense of motivation is directly connected to your overall wellbeing, a positive frame of mind will drive you to exercise beyond your perceived physical limits by pushing a little harder.
In addition, you are more inclined to try something new and explore the physical activities which can enrich your life, making you fitter, healthier and happier etc.

It all starts with a thought, and that thought is determined, or rather controlled, by your sense of wellbeing

Five positive effect of Wellbeing on exercise;

1. Increases your desire to exercise
2. Enhances your physical endurance
3. State of mind readies you for competition
4. Increases personal resolve
5. Mind over matter, think it and do it

External factors to well-being

The world is diverse and infinitely complex, all thanks to your incalculable range of personal experiences, it is due to this that the challenges faced by you are unique, how you perceive something can be totally different to how the person next to you perceives the exact same thing. What makes you laugh might offend them, neither of you is right or wrong to feel the way you do.

The thing is, nobody is born 'standard', however the world adopts a single solution methodology which we're all expected to conform to, i.e., as a child you're trained by to become a standardised responsible adult.

Some people are readily absorbed into the unified state, while you may not feel that the one-size approach works for you, it is this process which can be the cause for many feeling excluded, stressed and aggrieved.

Standardising people can be akin to forcing a square outlook into a circular society, something has to give.

In this section we will discuss the external factors that have an affect your positivity and well-being in general, there are of course as many factors to consider as there are grains of sand on every beach in the world, however I will stick to five of the major ones which might effect you.

Advertising
Family
Friends
Money
Work

Advertising

Direct and indirect, product placement and telephone harassment subjects us to advertising messages from all angles, they never switch off, they play on our fears, dreams, hopes, the promise of sex and the assurance of bliss, whiter teeth or the sports car you should have by now.

Advertising causes doubt, jealousy, animosity and a whole range of negative emotions driven by angst, cynicism and betrayal... That body spray didn't make me irresistible or that bra didn't make me feel as uplifted as promised.

The effects of advertising has gone from the mainstream and into your personal life, after switching off the TV, turning down the radio and throwing away the magazines the advertising persists, now it's involved in your chats with your friends via a social media platform which knows your likes and dislikes.

Advertising has a serious and relentless effect on life, it drives the consumer beast within, the more you surrender, the more you give, the more it effects you, this creates addictions, whether fast food (or any food), gambling, drinking, smoking (where sneakily product placed) and of course drug addiction to get away from the relentless noise.

By Mark McIntyre

Remember that advertisers are playing a game.
You are mostly powerless in this day and age to avoid
the marketing drive of those wanting you to buy, but
you can choose to disregard it.

Becoming immune to advertising requires the
understanding that it's a game, by training yourself that
their messages are worthless, contrived and controlling
you can break free and live in the confidence that you
understand the world with a little more clarity.

Family

Family plays a significant role and can be the major factor in your overall sense of wellbeing.
It is in your inherent nature to be flawless, we are born as a blank canvass with the potential to be nurtured into a masterpiece and your family are the paint and brushes.

If like me, your childhood years were somewhat complex and challenging, then you have a tough call to make, it can only be you who does this... do you choose to retain the chaotic image painted by those who vandalised the canvass or do you whitewash it all and start again, entrusting friends with the paint and brushes instead?

Family is important and under ideal conditions offers you security, encouragement and greater confidence, in addition to well being and positivity.

You might be of the belief that you're stuck with people who offer you nothing but negativity on the premise that blood is thicker than water or the saying that you can't choose your family but you can choose your friends etc.

Friends

You choose your friends on the basis that they add something to your life, whether it's understanding, encouragement, humour, help or common interests in general.

These days, your friends come in categories, they are favourites and time-lined, some are face to face friends while others remain in the digital ether, popping up with updates which are innate, ignored or deleted.

Modern society has you tagging and not discussing, sharing online but not sharing time together, but in some way, you still choose...

Friends play a vital role in persuading you, convincing you and showing you, they mould your personality and either contribute or take away... you know, the ones who constantly complain and feel as though they drain you and them who are forever bubbly and entertain you.

A friend of mine, who was a real gem, once said that she liked waterfalls but hated drains, I didn't have the faintest idea what she was talking about until I noticed that the reason she was so positive all the time was because she surrounded herself with positive people...

Do this yourself, look at couples and groups (but don't stare, it's weird), you will often find that negatives often stay around negatives and positives stay with positives, which group look more content and happy?

The crux of this is that you become shaped by those who influence you, if you feel negative more than you like, then look at the company you keep.

As highlighted elsewhere, joining social groups gives you instant access to people who you have some commonality with, if you introduce yourself to more positive influences in your life, you might become more positive in life.

Money

Money makes the world go round but while it allows you to buy things that make you happy, it won't in itself bring happiness, this is a highly contradictory statement which might be why you may feel conflicted about it.

It has always seemed to me, to be overly simplistic to say that an excess of money makes you unhappy, it might be more useful to understand your relationship with money and your internal and external influencers to well-being.

It seems we value people's monetary contribution more than anything else, Van Gough was considered crazy, his work going unappreciated throughout his life, it was only once a monetary value was placed on his work did people, posthumously value him as a person and as someone who contributed to society as a whole.

In my personal opinion, a society which values money above all else is seriously and irretrievably flawed.

Money is a social driver, we live in a society where money talks, it is the accepted global mark of success, a system whereby class is asserted and the currency of influence is spent.

We're conditioned by advertising and the fairy tales that money and greed can be good.

Let's take a look at life from the perspective of you being an Olympic 100m sprinter;

The gold medal is the prime driver (motivator) Would you still run the race if you were awarded the gold medal prior to running the 100m sprint?

What I'm getting at is money is the carrot (or stick) in life, it is a goal, a powerful motivator for many, or merely a means to an end for the rest.

Whatever your conviction and ambition, money requires personal drive, creativity, resolve and determination in order to collect it, remove that motivation and life seems somewhat empty.
It is often this that causes many of the (suddenly) wealthy to lose the plot and their personal direction as they already have the gold medal and all those years of preparation.

Given that money or medals are the end result, by bypassing the journey to the materialistic reward the foundation to who you are is removed, the structure of your life damaged.

Money can make you happy provided it is not used to bypass experiences that help you to grow.

The same can be said of the welfare system;
In some cases the system can become the death blow to personal determination and ambition.

Money can do tremendous good, if you have a sudden excess then why not put some to good use, develop a new purpose in life, new challenges and a new direction.
If money is short, then take a look at how much you invest in material possessions compared to an investment in yourself, learning, travel and general personal development.

If money makes you happy, then good, but look at additional routes to happiness, hanging onto money as an exclusive source of personal satisfaction is false, it can be lost or taken away in a heartbeat.

Work

'The office' makes up 33% of your adult working life, more time is committed to working than any other single factor in life, you spend more time with work colleagues than with your own friends, family or personal quality time...

You spend more time at the desk than in bed, Infact, between work and sleep you really don't have much time for anything else...

If you love your job then great, infact, better than great, fantastic! You have the right job and vocation, on balance your life is likely a more positive experience overall.
Sometimes, people love their job because other elements in their life are lacking, that's possibly something for you to explore if you identify with this.

Work for most people brings you money and money is needed to pay the bills and to be valued by society, for this reason, the very thing that can form you, improve you, motivate you and influence all aspects of what makes you, is merely done in the pursuit of wealth.

If your work is making you unhappy, dissatisfied and anxious, stressed or any other range of negative emotions then you have to ask yourself if that job is worthy of you.

I'm not about to say that you must quit work and live in tent somewhere (good idea though)

Instead, be proactive, you can you change anything, especially your approach to work culture, for instance, many roles allow flexible working including working from home and setting your own hours etc.

If you are having issues with work then is your boss aware?
Are you trying too hard to impress?
By that I mean taking work home in order to win favour etc, bare in mind that you're already losing 33% of your life to work, why lose even more?

If all else fails, look at self employment or even write a book.
You're only ever a slave to the conditions you set for yourself.

Enjoy your freedom of self determination, you always have a choice.

Your inner well-being

Newspapers will often seem outraged that society has become shallow, mooting examples of negative eating habits and the tragedy concerning the decline of mental health in society as a whole.

On the next page they highlight the microscopic flaws on a celebrity's skin or facial features that they would change if they had the money. The mixed messages in the printed press, TV news, docu-soaps and movies are inadvertently mixed at best, or deliberately designed to damage at worst. The end result is that many internal feelings can be greatly amplified, for better or worse, by what you choose to view.

Remember that the internal effects of confidence are 100% under your control, by doing something different today you can start to take full control back.

These are the five of the main internal drivers which control your inner well-being;

Anxious feelings
Confidence
Emotional barriers
Fear
Physical appearance

Anxious feelings

Anxiety can make you feel as though your stomach is permanently knotted in anticipation of an event.

It is a hormonal response based on the fight or flight reflex, this can be good, it keeps you on your toes, i.e. before a job interview, a strenuous physical task or being picked out of an audience etc.

If you feel anxious prior to such events but okay once it has passed, then you can relax, it's a completely normal reaction.

It can be all too easy to be talked into believing (by well intentioned people on the whole) that this is a big issue requiring intervention in pill form.

If however you feel an almost continuous sense of anxiety then you could try to find the triggers which set off your anxiety and then developing coping mechanisms to overcome anxiety. This is key.

Overcoming anxiety can come from improved nutrition, getting out, joining common interest groups etc.

Counselling can help too.

Confidence

It is said that some people are born that way, while others need to strive to attain that, I'm not so sure how valid that statement is.

Confidence is fed from the vast range of factors that have formed you throughout your life so far.

Your upbringing plays a significant role in your lifelong confidence levels, some people will battle against adverse conditions while others are pulled into the mire of self doubt, often created by those who should have been be much more supportive earlier on.

Confidence can also be derived by personal achievements, often as perceived by others around you, if you made the best paper aeroplane in the world and all around you gave praise then this would boost your confidence.
If however you won gold medals at the Olympics yet all around you relentlessly picked faults, then this could shatter your confidence.

So it could be said that confidence is derived from approval, helping someone build their confidence can therefore be achieved by giving approval, and as they feel valued, they in turn approve of other peoples accomplishments and efforts.

This is how I interpret Gandhi's '*Be the change you want to see in the world*'. That being, you will become more confident as a direct consequence of lifting others.

Be the example.

If you feel that you lack confidence then joining an activity group, art class perhaps and something that involves a brand new circle of friends, can help more than anything else.

While there, complement other students, you will, through mutual understand elevate each others confidence levels.

Emotional barriers

These are formed on the basis of insecurities and built on negatives, while barriers may seem to be a useful way to protect yourself from the pain of love lost or trust in general.

The barriers which are built are two way, they keep all the risky influences at bay, but they also keep you as a prisoner to your insecurities.

These barriers can be highly detrimental in the longer term.

There are plenty of analogies to counter the forming of barriers;
if you fall off a bike then you get back on the saddle and cycle off.
In the same way, if something goes wrong in life try to learn from it and move on, there are many groups that you join to help.

Again, good diet and exercise are excellent natural methods of overcoming emotional trauma.

Instead of building barriers, build a new social outlook, change your friends, move in different circles, break old habits and meet the best people for you, not the ones from habit.

By Mark McIntyre   156

Fear

Terrorism, attack, muggings, losing, betrayal, physical harm, expecting the worst, opinions, twisted facts, the weather, storms, flying, spiders, horror, strangers and so much more.

Fear covers more than the fear of your physical condition or safety (anxiety), it covers more than the fear of making a fool of yourself.
Instead, fear is often thrown at you as a norm, it is an expectation that you should be fearful, but there's something to remove fear, simply buy this, or that.
Yes, fear is used as a sales tool.

Essentially, fear is a control mechanism, whether prescribed mentally through the media or physically by confrontation.
Of course, the sense of fear can be a good thing, it is a self preservation mechanism to promote a longer life, ie, you will drive more carefully in the dark and won't put your hand in the fire etc. It keeps you from harms-way.

There are ways to be less fearful, this is to detune yourself from the negatives of externally induced fear, so unplug the TV, close down the computer and avoid the press for a week and see what happens to fear and indeed many of the elements which conspire to suppress your positivity.

Physical appearance

In many cases, physical appearance can indicate how you feel about yourself. There seems to be a synergy of the more positive the person the better the posture, as such, the less positive the worse the posture becomes.

As posture and positivity seem linked in this way, it is reasonable to say that if you're feeling negative then trick your inner self into feeling positive by actively improving your posture. (Give it a go)

This one small step can become a solid start to change.
There are other factors too, including how you view your body shape.
Think why you view your shape the way you do, if you conclude that it will be beneficial to you for a range of reasons, including increasing energy, fitness and functional abilities then seek ways to make the changes.

The A to Z to positivity

Read through the A-Z list for ideas and methods for you to promote enhanced positivity and well-being.

As with the rest of the book, take the elements that appeal to you, not all of them will, but here goes…

Age is not a limiting factor to any personal goal

Breakfast should be a fulfilling experience and worth getting out of bed for

Convenience food often comes with a delayed inconvenient price

Do something different today, no matter how minor the action.
Everyone has flaws, accept that and judge lightly

Fresh fruit and veg makes everything better

Give something to a random person (money, compliments, time etc)

Hating and hateful thoughts will twist your soul and hurt you more.

Inject some more fun into your life, whether it's a video game or holiday.

Join an activity group - musical, fitness, art class or paint-balling; it's social and can lift you.

KBO - Keep buggering on! It's the only way you will get there.

Let go of negative feelings and what do you have left?

Make something, anything, it gives the sense of a job well done

Never say never - bridges have odd names

Open yourself to new possibilities

Proactive in action, positive in result

Quiet time to focus and listen to your inner thoughts

Running releases endorphins, sitting suppresses them

Sweating, grunting and groaning during intense physical activity makes it better

Trying and failing is better than inaction and complaining

Undermining others only shafts yourself

Venom kills - be the antidote

When going through hell, don't stop

Xenodochial actions are returned ten fold

You can only start by taking that first tentative step

Zzzz's are important, rest well, recharge and rejuvenate

Extras

Positivity weekly groups

Groups offer a number of tremendous benefits in becoming more confident and positive, especially if you can't attend personal coaching sessions due to any number of factors, including the money factor.

By their very nature, the groups are sociable and welcoming; those people attending tend to be open minded with less of a propensity to judge others.

Essentially, you're with a group of people who all have something in common, so this commonality is shared, this can help you make new friends and connections, driving your positivity journey further.

It's perfect for anyone wishing to build confidence and positivity while seeking to control weight Check out the details…

www.positivelyhealthierlifestylecoaching.co.uk

www.Facebook.com/PositivelyConfident

Personal Coaching

Personal positivity coaching can have a profoundly positive effect on your, outlook, well-being and ability to live the life you want to live for yourself.

If you would like to contact me, then you will pleased to know that I'm able to provide a personal coaching service to you, wherever you are; Ideally in person, failing that, via email, text, phone or Skype etc.

The Personal coaching that I offer is dynamic, allowing you to explore more of the factors that enhance all the elements in helping you become more positive for life.

Book me via the website here.

www.positivelyhealthierlifestylecoaching.co.uk

www.Facebook.com/PositivelyConfident

Your feedback

Thank you for having read through this book, I hope you have gained something from it that can help you becoming a more positive person.

If you have a question about the book or have any feedback about what you have read and how it relates to you then do feel free to drop me a line.

I will get back to you as soon as I can.

Mark McIntyre

Freedom@positivelyhealthierlifestylecoaching.co.uk

CPSIA information can be obtained
at www.ICGtesting.com
Printed in the USA
LVOW13s1628270717
542867LV00012B/1174/P

9 781482 357332